FAITH

The Grace of
FAITH

Pastor William R. Grimbol

ALPHA

A Pearson Education Company

This book is dedicated to my friend and partner in ministry, Jordan Eichorn, for being such a remarkable source and inspiration of faith.

International Standard Book Number: 0-02-864428-X

Library of Congress Catalog Card Number: 2002111654

04 03 02   8 7 6 5 4 3 2 1

Interpretation of the printing code: The rightmost number of the first series of numbers is the year of the book's printing; the rightmost number of the second series of numbers is the number of the book's printing. For example, a printing code of 02-1 shows that the first printing occurred in 2002.

Printed in the United States of America

For marketing and publicity, please call: 317-581-3722

The publisher offers discounts on this book when ordered in quantity for bulk purchases and special sales.

For sales within the United States, please contact: Corporate and Government Sales, 1-800-382-3419 or corpsales@pearsontechgroup.com

Outside the United States, please contact: International Sales, 317-581-3793 or international@pearsontechgroup.com

Contents

Introduction

Faith. It is not a doctrine or dogma. It is not defined or confined by rule, regulation, or ritual. There are not those who have it and those who do not. We all have it. It is in our blood. It is our original blessing. It is as natural to us as breathing. It is the source of our being.

Faith. There is no right faith or wrong faith. There is no ranking of faith. There is no such thing as a superior or inferior faith. There is nobody closer to God than we are. There is only the reality of the presence. It is up to us to notice. Faith is paying attention.

Faith. It is an instinct, an intuition, a holy hunch. We know the truth when we hear it, see it, feel it, or experience it. We especially know the truth when we feel it in our bones. We get a goose bump or a lump in our throat. We are moved to tears or left dumbstruck. A shiver scoots up and down our spine. Our bodies are ceaselessly informing us of the will of God.

Some of us believe we have no faith at all. Some of us may believe but are not sure it matters much. Many of us question the relevance of our religious upbringing.

We may have spiritual roots, but they do not go deep. There are those who keep their faith tidy. Life's mysteries and questions are kept neatly in compartments, unstained by doubt. There are a few who have a firm, fine, and simple faith, strong as rock, fierce as a mother's love.

But all of us have lost our faith at some point. We have all known bitter times when God appeared to be against us. We have all had our faith shattered by loss. No matter how strong our faith, we have all known times when our belief simply wilted and withered and blew away.

How is it then that we lose faith? Can it be destroyed? Does it just wander off or flee like a bandit into the night?

Our faith is there, out in the open. It isn't hidden. It is never far. It is always waiting for a visit. It may be in the shadows or right before our eyes. It may come in a flash or a glance or a glimpse. It may poke or prod us or offer the comfort of a caress. At times it begs for attention, pleads for trust, or whispers "sweet everythings" in our ears. At all times faith is calling us back home to God.

In this little book we will explore some of the ways our world encourages us to lose faith. We will examine how we bury faith under busyness and boredom; how the worship of money sells the soul; how we suffocate our spirits by robbing them of the fresh air of pleasure and play; and how we lose contact with our longing and desires and, in so doing, become alienated from God.

We will learn of successful spiritual strategies for finding, uncovering, and recovering faith. We will focus on living our faith. Putting faith into practice. Walking the walk. Integrating faith into our daily lives. Making hope happen. Living in love. Being like gods. Claiming our heritage as God's beloved.

Acknowledgments

Good books are grown. They must be carefully sown, nurtured and nourished, protected and defended. They might even require a scarecrow. Good books require good gardening—which means good gardeners.

I wish to thank Randy Ladenheim-Gil for sowing the seeds of this project in good soil as well as watering and fertilizing my spirit as needed.

My gratitude to Nancy Lewis and Christy Wagner for carefully weeding and pruning the manuscript. Editing is the process we all wish to avoid, yet the one that yields the harvest of a good book.

And, once again, an affirmation to Marie Butler-Knight for fencing in this book and enabling it to safely grow.

To you all—seen and unseen, known and unknown—I hope you enjoy the blossoms. I think they are beautiful. I hope you do as well. It makes quite the bouquet.

A Maze

*The feeling of being hurried is not usually the
result of living a full life and having no time.
It is, rather, born of a vague fear that we are
wasting our life.*

—Eric Hoffer

This past fall I took my Club 456—fourth, fifth, and
sixth graders—to a corn maze on a farm in Bridge-
hampton, New York. The kids were enthusiastic, assur-
ing me that they would conquer the maze in mere
minutes. At first it was fun, winding our way in and
out, getting blocked, making a correct turn. But as the
"game" went on, I saw worry creep across many of the
kid's faces. They stuck closer to me. One child was
attached to my hip and was near panic.

We were sweating. We itched. We felt hopelessly lost
much of the time. We just kept moving. When Andrew
shouted, "I see the way out!" my herd raced out of there
as if escaping a fire. Though they whooped and cheered,

I asked, "Shall we do it again?" "No way!" came back the chant. They had had more than enough.

In many respects, we adults live our lives as if we are trapped in a maze—a maze of expectations, a maze of duties and obligations, a maze of keeping everyone happy. We aren't sure if we are headed in the right direction, and there is no one to ask for directions. We are afraid of being trapped. We feel hopelessly stuck, like we are marching in place in quicksand. So we just keep on moving.

The problem with this kind of movement is that everything becomes a blur. Our world tells us that this blur is a sign of our success, the busier, the better. The faster we move, the more important we are. We are the jet set. At the end of each day we can barely recall the day's events. We just know that we got through our checklist. There's one big problem, though—ourselves and God were not on the checklist.

Life in a maze is deadly. There is little life there. No amazement. No time to laugh, play, or love. There is no joy. There is just the busyness. The mind grows numb. The heart turns callused. The soul runs for cover. Our faith is lost.

Life in a maze is the formula for burnout. Burnout is when life's obligations and duties keep increasing, while the rewards and gratifications decrease. Burnout is when the fire in our hearth goes out. The soul grows cold. The warmth and energy are gone. All flames of excitement and enthusiasm have been extinguished.

Life in a maze has an insane goal—getting out of the maze, escaping, as if life were a prison or an endurance test that nobody is expected to pass. Those in the maze try to give one another looks of assurance, the comfort of knowing that at some point they will get out. The looks offer compassion but no hope.

The tragedy is that the real living is all taking place outside the maze. Even my kids were smart enough to feel no need to reenter the maze. Sadly, most of us go back again and again. The world tells us that the maze is reality, a requirement of adult living. We are bombarded with the notion that in the maze we will make a name for ourselves. The truth is that in the maze we lose our identities. We become numbers. We become a blur.

There is no faith to be found in the maze. Faith tells us that all maze movement leads to a dead-end. Faith reminds us that God calls us to wander outside the walls.

Faith invites us to stroll in lush valleys and climb lovely peaks.

Faith is not lost in the blur. Faith is clarity. Faith has a clear message about living in a maze.

Get Out!

Finding faith will require us to get out of the maze— if not permanently, as often as we can. We will need to make choices to get out. These choices will require putting ourselves and God back on our checklists. We will need to choose some down time, which, ironically, brings us back up. We will need to do nothing, which, ironically, frees us to be everything God would want us to be. We will need to play, which, ironically, re-creates us.

Finding faith is choosing another path. It is indeed the road less traveled. It is the way of the heart. It is an expressway to freedom. The maze is all controlled and chained movement. Faith is the wild roaming of maturation—spirituality. Spirituality and maturation are traveling partners.

One sure way to end the blur of busyness is to stop. Cease. Stand still. Be still. Be quiet. It sounds so simple because it is. Most true faith begins with stop. We stop trying to be in charge. We stop trying to be in control.

We stop trying to do God's work. We let go. We wave the white flag. We surrender.

The maze offers us nothing—nothing that matters or lasts, nothing eternal. Eternal things are all found outside the maze. Outside we learn how to stand still and receive. We must empty ourselves in order to be filled. We lose our lives in order to find them. Receiving is the posture and activity of faith.

Don't Go In!

Living in a maze becomes addictive. The longer we spend in the maze, the outside, like our insides, all becomes a blur. We forget the beauty outside. We lose the pleasure of wandering. We are isolated and alone. So when we are offered one more run through the maze, or even a new maze to navigate, we leap at the chance. We are certain that *this* time the maze will yield the success and happiness it has promised. It never does.

The world tells us that the faster we run the maze, the sooner we can get out. The opposite is true. The more and faster we run, the more addicted we become. The run is all we know. The thought of a leisurely stroll outside creates enormous anxiety. What will we feel? What will we think about? What will we say? Will anybody out there love us? It is just easier to stick with what we know—the maze.

Before Moses led the Jews on the Exodus, the Jews were slaves who toiled tirelessly in a brickyard. The work was back- and soul-breaking. What most do not realize is that many Jews chose not to follow Moses. They chose life in the brickyard. Why? It offered the illusion of safety and security. It appeared to be less risky. It was familiar and anxiety-free.

Many of us toil like slaves in the brickyard, afraid to leave, anxious about the enormous desert that awaits our wandering, frightened of freedom, with our faith in the Promised Land having all but evaporated. There is nothing but the bricks ... the bucks.

Go Slow, and Look Up!

It is not easy to get out of the maze. All our lives will, at times, feel like a maze. We all have spent a good chunk of time in a maze. If we can't get out, then what? I suggest two things: Go slow, and look up.

One clear lesson the kids learned in the maze was that the slower we went, the faster we solved the puzzle of the maze. Going slow allowed us time to think, a chance to remember if we had been this way before. Those first crazy chaotic moments of running around the maze only got us hot and frustrated. Slowly but surely, we were able to make our way through the maze.

Looking up at the sky overhead reminded us that the maze was not all there is. We were not really trapped. There was always one way out. We could be lifted up and out. Faith is that lift. Faith moves us skyward.

We lose our faith by being too busy. Our busyness shapes our existence into a maze from which we believe we cannot escape. We feel trapped like rats, and as Lily Tomlin once wisely said, "Even if you win the rat race, you are still a rat!"

The Questions
How tired am I? Am I wasting my time? What am I sick and tired of doing and being?

The Prayer
O God, give me direction. Straighten my path. Let me clearly see the horizon. Let me slow down and savor the journey. Amen.

Out of Touch

Normal day, let me be aware of the treasure you are.
—*Mary Jean Irion*

We all have driven in fog. It is an eerie experience. We start slow, letting our eyes adjust to our limited vision. As our eyes adjust, we are tricked into thinking we can see better than we truly can. We accelerate. A car passes us. We speed up. An elderly lady with blue hair whizzes by. We near the actual speed limit. We try to look confident, but we are haunted by a nagging fear. The fog is as thick as Elmer's glue.

Suddenly, unexpectedly, dramatically, the fog lifts. We are stunned and relieved. We cannot believe how well we can see. We also cannot believe how poor our vision was just moments before. We recognize our confidence as an illusion. We realize the danger of having driven as though the fog did not exist. We are shocked by our poor judgment.

We will probably do the exact same thing the next time we drive in fog. We will pretend there is no fog. We will act as if we can see for miles rather than feet.

Many of us choose to live in a fog. We are unaware of our bodies. We have lost contact with our emotions. We pay little to no attention to our souls. We are out of touch with our selves, our world, and our God.

The fog is composed of many things. Busyness is certainly a major contributor. But there is also an ample portion of worry and fear. Grief forms a chunk, as do guilt and shame. There are also traces of anger and envy. Most of all, the fog is the result of trying to be in control. It is a pearl-white whirlwind of trying to be self-sufficient, or perfect, or both.

The fog first appears as a mist. It seems harmless. It is only as the fog builds in density that it becomes dangerous. So it is with our lives. The longer we avoid being aware of what our bodies are telling us, the more prone we are to injury or illness. The more detached we become from our feelings, the greater the chance they will fester or erupt. The farther removed we become from the spiritual realm, the more likely it is that we will suffer from depression or anxiety or become hopelessly mired in cynicism or apathy.

The fog keeps us from being aware or conscious. We fail to see the truth of our selves or our neighbor. We remain unconscious of our motivations or desires. We have no vision of where we would like to go or who we would like to become. We feel stranded. Stuck. We lose faith. Faith is having our eyes wide open. Faith is the freedom to move. This fog denies us the experience of either—awareness or movement.

Living in such a fog will ultimately prevent our maturation. We are unable to learn or grow. We cannot change. We take no risks. We dream no dreams. We grow weary of the routine but are comfortable in our ruts. The ruts, like shallow graves, keep us from being fully and honestly alive. We become deadened. Over time, the fog can become lethal.

Faith can lift this fog. Faith unleashes our senses. Faith frees us to move in all directions. Faith enables us to walk with confidence through our days. Assured of our path, we stride with conviction. We move forward, sure of our step.

How? How does faith lift us out of the fog? How can faith reestablish contact with our hearts, minds, bodies, and souls?

In Touch

Faith is a voice. It is a song of the heart, a conscience, a calling. It is a shouting stone, a speaking silence, the whisper on the wind. Faith speaks a core message. It has one primary lesson to teach. It begs us to pay attention, to take notice, to stay in touch.

Paying attention to our bodies is vital to faith. The body is one of God's best tutors. Often our body speaks softly, sending subtle messages. A headache or knot in our stomach may tell of a worry or fear. A stiff neck or shoulders might inform us we are carrying a burden or stress. Feeling faint might just mean we need to get away from some person or situation. Being tired all the time might point to being bored or blue.

At times the body shouts and even screams for attention. A cold or flu may finally get us the rest we need. An ulcer may be an incentive to change jobs. When we are sick and tired of being sick and tired, we may address an addiction that is digging our grave.

The body sends us daily messages about our balance. Balance is the key to a healthy body and life. If we lose our balance, we fall. We may fall hard or flat on our faces. If we are to pick ourselves up again, we will need our faith to be in focus. It is our faith that will right our lopsided lives. Faith centers us in God. Faith grounds us in grace. Faith creates a body at ease. Faith leaves our bodies with nothing more to say than a sigh of relief.

Our faith is a body of knowledge. The body knows what matters to us most. The body is in touch with the truth. When we hit bottom, it will take faith in God to restore our balance. When God is back on top, all is right with the world. God's place is not on the back burner. God needs to be up front. We need to be up front with God. This is the intimacy of true faith.

A Touching Moment

The first year following the loss of my wife Christine was such a fog, a big blur. It was hard to concentrate. It was difficult to focus. Each day began with a frenzy. As the day progressed, the chaos only worsened. It was like being captured on a merry-go-round. Daily I would wait for the spinning to stop. Sleep was the only relief.

I was badly out of balance. My head swarmed with mosquitoes of worry. My heart lay battered, bruised, and broken. My body was ravaged by aches and pains. I felt better when I was in my minister's uniform, but I was a wreck in my own skin. So … I stayed busy working. It was much easier playing God than admitting how much I needed God. Ironically, I was offering others faith at the very time I felt emptied of my own.

It was my son who snapped me out of it. He has never liked me in "ministry mode." He does not want a relationship with Rev. Grimbol. He wants his dad.

"How are you, Dad?"

"I am plugging along, Justin."

"How are you, Dad?"

"Well, Justin, I am doing the best I can."

"HOW ARE YOU, DAD?"

"Every night I still wait for her to come through the back door. I ache to hear her laugh. I want to give her a foot massage. I want to smell her hair and sleep like spoons." I wept.

Justin refused to indulge my fog of emotion. He demanded that I locate what I was feeling at that very moment. It was a touching moment, because it brought me back to my heart. My heart had been encased in this thick fog of grief. The only sound it made was a grunt or groan. Now it spoke in words—real words—giving expression to real feelings. It made an enormous difference.

As my feelings found a voice, so did my faith. I could hear God's condolences. I knew in my heart that my tears rolled down God's cheeks. I felt embraced. My pain diminished in size and intensity. When we lose contact with our hearts and our feelings, we have lost a vital lifeline. Emotions are God's vocabulary. They speak the language of love and maturation. They reveal God's call.

To be in touch with our hearts is to feel the rhythm of life, the pulse of God. So much of feeling good is about *feeling,* period. To be fully alive is to feel free to feel. Feelings are the signs and symbols of faith. Feelings are a primary means of contact with God.

Deeply Touched

The soul is the spirit, the seat of faith, the window through which we look to God.

The soul is real. The spirit requires time and attention. We need to deepen our faith. How? We ponder. We wonder. We think deep thoughts. We feel things passionately. We fight for what we believe. We stand up for our convictions. We give voice to our dreams. We actualize our vision. We write a fifth gospel with our lives.

Life wants to touch us deeply. We need to touch life deeply. We must dive into the day. We must dig into the matters of the heart. We must decide to be fully awake. The spiritual life is not lived on the surface. It is found in the depths of our being. It is located at our roots. Faith can never be shallow. It cannot run or hide from life or from the world.

A deep faith is one that is immersed in living, never afraid of being buried. We swim in an ocean of grace, never afraid of drowning. We walk on solid ground. A deep faith plunges into life's waters. A deep faith gets its hands dirty in the mud of the world. A deep faith is lived in this rhythm of diving and digging, getting dirty and being cleaned.

The Questions
When was I last deeply touched by life? How did I feel? How am I feeling now? What are the differences?

The Prayer
O God, pry me open. Teach me to receive. Pour out upon me the miracle and madness of the day. Let me cup it with tender hands. Let me call it a gift. Let me be gifted in its use. Amen.

Dead Certain

*He has made everything beautiful in its time;
also he has put eternity into man's mind, yet
so that he cannot find out what God has done
from the beginning to the end.*

—*Ecclesiastes 3:11*

Faith is not answers. Faith is not facts. Faith is not a certainty. If it were, we would merely call it knowledge. Faith implies a risk. The risk is in trusting your heart. The risk is taking a leap. This leap of faith is the primary movement of the human spirit as it chases the Divine Spirit.

What will inspire us to take this leap? Questions. It is the art of questioning. It is diving into the center of life's biggest questions:

- Who am I?
- What is my calling?
- Where will I find true love?
- When is it time to say good-bye?
- Why do we die?
- How can I make a difference?

Questions move us. They make us think. They force us to feel. They excite our souls. They ignite our leaping abilities.

Questions infest life. We see them in a look. We hear them in a moan. We touch them in the clasp of a hand. We taste them in the bitterness or sweetness in our stomachs. We experience them each and every time we choose to be aware. It is not possible to be fully alive and not be confronted by life's questions. Questions are at life's core. They are the beat of life's heart.

A good question brings us face-to-face with mystery. Mystery is not the absence of faith, but its essence. Mystery is the home of miracles. It is the dwelling place of hope. It is the catalyst for maturation—the movement of the spirit. Mystery leaves us in awe. It humbles us. It drives us to our knees. From our knees we can see that we are not God. From our knees we also gain insight into the overwhelming love of God.

Faith is nourished by mystery. Faith is inhabited by mystery. Faith rides on the wings of mystery. A mystery waves its wand, and thousands of bubbling questions float in the air. Each bubble is a universe; dancing on the air haunts us with wonder. We *ooh* and *ahh* as they spin. Though they may quickly explode and vanish before our eyes, the joy they emit lasts and lasts.

Without Question

A faith without questions is a blind faith. To speak of faith as a certainty robs the faith of its molten power. Dead certainty is just that—dead. To be dead certain is the choice to stop learning or maturing. It is a refusal to live in an ever-changing world. It is a denial of our humanity. A human being questions. It is our nature. It is a divinely planted instinct.

Doubt does not diminish faith. Doubt enhances faith. It deepens faith. It disciplines faith. It carries with it the demand for maturity. It challenges us to become more than we dream. It lifts us up to new heights. It hands us over to God.

Blind faith goes nowhere. It is stuck. It cannot serve anyone. It makes no sacrifices. It offers no love or forgiveness. It neither pursues justice nor practices peace. It just sits there and brags about having found the answer. The answer is repeated again and again, like a magical mantra. The words themselves become hollow as we soon realize they make no real difference in the way we live. In the end, they are just that—only words.

Blind faith cannot walk the walk. It can only talk. And talk. And talk ….

The Know-It-All

Is there anything worse than a know-it-all? Imagine being stuck on the proverbial desert island with someone who has all the answers. No questions. No doubts. No mystery. Somebody who would just go on and on and on about how his answers are the right answers, the *only* answers. The island's air would soon become polluted by a motor mouth who never runs out of gas. It would become harder and harder to breathe. We would start to gag. We need fresh air. What freshens spiritual air is questions and mysteries, even miracles.

The religious know-it-all is the worst. He believes he has God in his hip pocket. He is convinced that he not only has all the answers, but also a stranglehold on the truth. He cannot just talk, he preaches. His sermons seldom contain much more than bumper-sticker slogans tied together by a thick rope of righteousness. He smiles and acts as if he is listening, but it is all an act. His mind, like his faith, is all made up. It is faith in a box. If we want it we must buy the whole package. Each box is the same. No mystery here.

Killing Miracles

A faith without questions, a faith without doubts, a faith that contains no mystery is ultimately a faith without awe, reverence, miracle, or worship. We have all had our miracle moments or experiences. Can we box them up? Can we explain them? Should we even try? Well, we may attempt to share our miraculous events, but we know that the telling will never fully capture the experience. We know in our hearts that no words can bring a miracle back to life. In fact, most of the time words kill a miracle.

I remember my fifth-grade teacher showing us a firefly in a fruit jar. He explained exactly how the firefly made his light. His words spoiled the whole experience. Up until that point, fireflies were wondrous creatures whose mysterious light dotted many a magical summer night. Now they were just bugs. Fireflies in a fruit jar lose all of their glow.

I feel awe for the universe because its dimensions exhaust my mind. I feel reverence for the love I have for my son because I cannot fathom its depths. I worship a God I feel intimate with and close enough to to call friend, but one I often cannot grasp. The miracle of life is a daily event. I cannot contain all its wonders. I cannot even imagine the love that authored Creation, the setting of a sun, the flight of a bird, the giggles of kids playing, a first snowfall, the touch of a familiar hand, or the smell of a lilac. They all take my breath away. They leave me dumbstruck.

The Questions
Which questions most haunt my days? What do I find breathtaking and mysterious? For what am I in awe? What do I believe is worthy of worship?

The Prayer
O God, let me joyfully ask the questions. Strengthen my faith so that I might by embraced by the mystery. Embolden me that I might follow stars without knowing why. Amen.

Bored Stiff

Is not life a hundred times too short
for us to bore ourselves.
—Friedrich Nietzsche

It is everywhere these days. I see it on blank faces. I hear it in monotone voices. I experience it as a lack of energy, enthusiasm, and excitement. There is a listlessness that coats our culture. We walk with a limp. We speak of progress but are clueless as to where we are going or why. We act self-assured, but our pores ooze with worry. We seek to impress others with our got-it-together image yet frequently feel like we are falling apart.

What is this curious phenomenon? I believe it is boredom. I believe we are a culture that is bored to death with living a lie. The lie is mostly about money and greed. Money is our God. We won't admit it. We futilely try to talk our way out of it. We offer pathetic excuses. We rationalize to the hilt. I have even heard television evangelists say, "God wants us to have an abundant life," as if God meant money and stuff by abundance.

Our society is possessed with possessions, addicted to accumulation. American capitalism is built on a lie. The lie is making us believe we need things we do not need. It may work, and it may create work, but it is still a lie. Greed is our primary sin. We never have enough. We want more. We want bigger. We want faster. We want whatever they have. This mad chase after money destroys faith and creates empty lives.

If we can admit it, the pursuit of the good life in America has little or nothing to do with goodness. There is no time for a good conversation. There is little energy to build a good marriage or home. Our kids are often spoiled rotten—which means they have gone bad. They are not evil; they simply lack purpose or hope. Being a good neighbor is out of style. We have gone from being a nation with front porches to welcome neighbors in, to a nation of big fences to keep the neighbors out. We have no time or inclination to serve others. We ask what's in it for us. God is spoken of as a Thanksgiving table grace or on a seasonal visit to church or synagogue.

It is the absence of goodness that creates the boredom. Life without genuine goodness feels bad. Feeling bad is doing nothing that matters. Feeling bad is being stale and stagnant. A decadent culture creates a deadening lifestyle. Every major religion rightfully warns of the potential evil of money. The evil, as we know, is not the money itself, but the all-consuming passion to have it. It is the crazy belief that without it we are nothing. It is the absurd notion that we are what we own. This nonsense results in living what we know to be a lie, and as the lie grows, so does the deadly boredom.

Trivial Pursuits

When the good life has nothing to do with goodness, our lives become no more than trivial pursuits. We spend hours doing jobs we either hate or endure. We feel chained to a clock. Our work feels disconnected from our souls. We could care less about what we create. We are ruled by a technology that is out of our control. Our dreams decay. Our longings wither and fade. We simply go through the motions. We disappear. We are bored stiff.

Faith is never a trivial pursuit. Faith targets only that which matters. Faith is a matter of ultimate importance. Faith focuses on that which has eternal value—our relationships, our service to others, our efforts to build the Kingdom of God on this earth, our passion and compassion. Faith is inextricably bonded to our longings. The work of faith is loving and forgiving.

Faith considers money trivial. Yes, we do have to make a living. Yes, we need food and clothing and shelter. No, we do not need a house with five bathrooms. No, we do not need a closet full of clothes we never wear. No, we do not need a garage filled with adult toys. Faith confronts the lie. Faith confirms what is necessity and what is luxury. Faith chooses simplicity. Faith decides on less.

Bad News

If you want to have a bad day, just start by listening to the news. The news is overwhelming. It is a real blow to hope. By the end of hearing a seemingly endless litany of violence and crisis and catastrophe, our souls are numb. We stagger into our day. Our energy is depleted. Our hope drains away. Our attitude becomes sour. Boredom sets in. We won't make a dent of difference anyway.

We live in a culture that worships celebrities. A celebrity is someone who is known for being known. We pay our highest salaries to those who entertain us. We watch countless talk shows filled with movie or sports stars, never asking if they have anything of value to say. Our airwaves are saturated with shows displaying humanity at its worst. The more unbelievable the story, the more likely it will make it into our living room. Tabloid journalism is now a staple of our news networks and our prime-time television fare.

This is another lie in which we have been caught. Bad news is ultimately not entertaining. It is mind-numbing. It is soul-selling. It is spirit-killing. When we fill our minds with junk, our hearts with hate, and our souls with silliness, we are bound to be bored stiff.

Bad news is about bad people. Bad news is about bad people doing bad things. Bad news is a culture that has gone bad. Bad news has no room for goodness. Bad news has no interest in a good person, a good story, or even a good conversation. Bad news enjoys people eating maggots for money, politicians screaming at one another, or drunken teenage girls baring their breasts. Ironically, most bad news isn't newsworthy at all.

The Good Life

The genuine good life is all about goodness. It is about good people living good lives. It is about good neighbors. It is about doing good and being good.

Yes, I am encouraging us to be do-gooders. Most of the good we do is rooted in having faith in being good. Be kind. Be patient. Be generous. Be gentle. Be positive.

Be compassionate. Be genuine. When we choose to be a good person, the acts of goodness will naturally follow. If we believe in goodness, it forms the base of our faith. Then we can construct lives of good deeds. Brick by good-deed brick, we will build God's Kingdom on earth.

The Questions
When and with whom am I most bored? Why? Can this change? How must I change?

The Prayer
O God, why do we choose boredom? Why do we focus so much energy on trivialities? Why do we bathe ourselves in bad news? Why are we so easily enslaved to money? Free us to choose goodness. Free us to pursue real riches. Free us to follow your path to the genuine good life. Amen.

Homeless and Anonymous

*A man travels the world over in search of
what he needs and returns home to find it.*

—George Moore

I have a great new group at my church called The
Young at Heart Club. You must be 55 years old or older
to be in this club. The only other requirement for mem-
bership is loving to eat and appreciating the van-driving
skills of your Ralph Kramden–look-alike pastor.

I recently took the gang into New York City to have
lunch and see a movie. We decided to walk the few
blocks from the restaurant to the movie theater. It was a
lovely spring day, and the air felt soft and warm. Our
short pilgrimage took us past at least a half dozen homeless people. I noticed that my folks averted their eyes.
They simply moved toward the curb and went past as if
they were oblivious to the problems of those people.

Not one person stopped to read a sign or offer a buck or a word of hello.

We saw the film *Monster's Ball,* for which Halle Berry won an Oscar for Best Actress. It was my selection. It was an excellent movie but quite disturbing. The racism and sex were both ample and graphic. As the van waddled onto the freeway, I listened to my passengers chatter about how unsettling they found the film. A few even sounded upset. The sex was clearly over the top for two senior ladies. All agreed the film was worthy of viewing, but they were clearly distressed by some of its contents.

Though I chose to say nothing, I was fascinated by our group's lack of upset over the sight of the homeless but their being flustered response to the film. How had these homeless become invisible to us? How were we Christians able to walk by so easily, as if these human beings did not exist? How and why had we been transformed into such callous creatures? I pondered these questions the remainder of the trek home.

This is what I concluded. We fear the homeless. We fear what they symbolize. They show us our greed in graphic detail. They are the acid test of faith. We also see ourselves in the homeless. Were we to look them in the eye, speak to them, or even reach out to touch them, we would experience our own state of spiritual homelessness. The homeless are our spiritual mirrors.

"Spiritual homelessness?" you ask. Yes. I think we are all homeless. Homelessness is the great spiritual malady of our times. Our New York City neighbors may lack for physical shelter, but we are missing the shelter of grace. We yearn for a deeper faith and a fuller relationship to God. We know in our heart of hearts that we have wandered far away from God. Our loss of faith stems from having missed the mark with our choices. If we feel distant to God, it is not God who has strayed.

Don't underestimate our spiritual pain. It may not cut as deep as being literally homeless, but it can be disabling. Think of Dorothy if she were permanently stuck in Oz. Think of ET being forced to live out his days in LA. Imagine the prodigal son never returning to the simple goodness of life on the farm. Without a spiritual home, our lives become tragedies.

Homesickness

I clearly remember my son Justin's first five letters from Camp Ballibay. They were written on his first five days away from home. I wept as I read each one. His pain had a taste—burnt. It had a smell—rancid. It had a touch—razor's edge. His words reduced his daddy to Jell-O. Justin's mother had to literally barricade me from getting in my car to go get him.

Homesickness is real. It is God-awful. Spiritual homesickness is just as real. When we lose faith, we have lost contact with home. God is home. When we dwell in God, we feel safe and secure. When we try to go it alone, we become anxious and arrogant—a miserable mix.

Our culture encourages us to run away from home. Why? By promising us that life away from home is more exciting. By telling us that we cannot be somebody until we leave. By blasting us with the message that our treasure can only be found outside the walls of home.

We can't go home again—the American mantra. In many respects it is true. Justin needed to adjust to being away from home, and Camp Ballibay did turn out to be a rewarding experience for him. We all need to leave our physical homes to mature. If we are to establish our identity and independence or be capable of the intimacy required of marriage and family, we can only do so having left home. In terms of our spiritual home, however, the opposite is true.

God is our spiritual home. We are God's creation, God's children, God's beloved. If we choose to separate from this love, we lose our center, our souls, and our connectedness to grace. The more we try to be in charge, in control, to go it alone, trying to prove our self-sufficiency, the more our spirits sag and suffer. Like a flower freshly cut, our beauty quickly fades. The browning begins. Soon the blossom has become a pile of withered petals.

Roots

One of the curses of our times and culture is the omnipresence of anxiety. We can feel the ground move beneath our feet. We have a queasiness in the pits of our stomachs. We become worrywarts. Our heads ache, and our limbs grow taut. We are waiting for the bomb to drop. We live as if there were no tomorrow. We grow wary of our neighbor. We build walls. We go into isolation. We know we are lonely, but we cannot admit it.

I suspect that anxiety is the result of being rootless. We do not feel anchored. Our faith is not strong enough to tether us to the day. We do not feel like we are in our lives but only orbit them. We float helplessly above. We want to land. We want to feel the firm ground beneath our feet. We want to walk. We want to move forward with our heads held high.

It is grace that grounds us. Faith in this grace enables us to land on solid ground. Faith serves as the catalyst for our movement. A strong faith walks the walk. Sometimes it may even strut or skip.

Loneliness

Ministers get lonely—like everybody else. Ministers don't admit to being lonely—like everybody else. Ministers won't discuss their loneliness—like everybody else.

If we are lonely, we are unpopular. If we are lonely, we must be a loser. If we are lonely, we may be unlovable. Since we do not wish to be any of these things, we hide our loneliness. We keep it secret. We let it eat away at our souls.

Loneliness is about not feeling understood. It is the result of feeling assumed or under appreciated. It is the product of a lack of intimacy. We may be well liked and surrounded by family and friends, and still feel miserably lonely. We are lonely when we feel unknown.

Loneliness is often accompanied with a sweeping sadness. We are in mourning. We lament the loss of our souls. We feel as though we have lived a lie. Our true selves have disappeared. We are no more than spiritual caricatures. We have no substance. No true being. We are just a rough sketch of our true selves.

Loneliness also makes us mad. We are angry at ourselves for sacrificing our vision and voice. We are irritated with others for not caring enough to know us. We feel ignored by friends and abandoned by God. The universe is coldly indifferent.

I believe that loneliness is *the* spiritual crisis of our time. It is certainly the primary issue I face in ministry. We have so much, but we lack that which would give our lives meaning and value—true friends and community. We need good neighbors and neighborhoods. We yearn for close-knit families. We desire spiritual communities that celebrate and grieve together.

We are a nation on anti-depressants. For the truly depressed, I think medication is a vital tool to good mental health. However, I suspect that much of our depression is loneliness. There is no pill we can swallow to replace a friend who respects and adores us.

Though loneliness is depressing, it is not depression. Loneliness is a spiritual malady. The cure for loneliness is contact, connectedness, and communication. It is knowing that you are not alone. It is feeling the presence of love. It is experiencing the presence of God. It is faith that keeps us focused on finding both.

Anonymous

Most of us spend our lives trying to make a name for ourselves. We scramble our way up the ladder of success, oblivious to whom we knock off in the process. We gorge on our piece of the pie. Many of us become addicts in the process. Our images begin to unravel. We hit bottom. We need help. To get help we must lose our names—become anonymous.

The estimates are staggering. Some 60 million Americans are involved in various anonymous organizations. Each anonymous gathering is an effort to battle an addiction—drugs, alcohol, overeating, gambling, or sex. I often think I could qualify for nearly every anonymous group out there. The only group I can't join is Paranoid's Anonymous, because they won't tell me where the meetings are.

Faith and faith gatherings also do battle with addictions. The addiction is to being in control and the love of money. Just like other addictions, these will rob us of our health, happiness, and spiritual home. We, too, can hit spiritual bottom and need help. Only this time we get to keep our names. We are not Sinners Anonymous. We are God's beloved, who never lose their names. As God's beloved we never need to worry about people knowing who we are, because we are God's.

The Questions
When, where, and with whom do I feel most at home? When, where, and with whom do I feel alienated? If God is my spiritual home, have I moved in? Why or why not?

The Prayer
O God, you have named us and claimed us as your own. Bring us home to your safe shelter. Offer us deep roots. Anchor us against the wild winds of the world's wisdom. May we always dwell in your Grace. Amen.

Angels and Aliens

*Be not forgetful to entertain strangers: for thereby
some have entertained angels unawares.*

—*Hebrews 13:2*

We live in anxious times. The world is stretched taut
by tension. Violence threatens from all sides. Terrorism
mocks our freedom. The globe is warming. The re-
sources are dwindling. Cancers creep under our skin.
Children dodge bullets in school. Teen suicide is a
bulging statistic. Addiction is today's idolatry. God
appears to have lost both a voice and vision.

At times I think of our world as an amusement park
ride—the one where a cylinder spins so fast, the riders
are plastered to the sides as the floor slips away. We have
grown dizzy. We are weary of the paralysis. We want a
floor beneath our feet. We want to feel safe and secure.
We want off this ride.

These are what I call the yearning years. We ache with
a desire to connect to a higher power. We tremble with

the need to locate a rhyme or reason. We search for meaning as if it were a lost child—our own lost child. Questions ring in our ears. "What is happening and why? Can we do anything about it? Is the world spinning hopelessly out of control?"

And so we look. We look up, down, in, and out. We look everywhere for the answer to our prayers. Unfortunately, some of the places we look can be dangerous. Some spots may advertise that they have faith to sell, but what they offer is cheap, shallow, and of no lasting value. It is important to remember that faith can never be bought. If it is being sold, if it carries a price tag, it is probably bogus.

Quick-Fix Religions

What is a quick-fix religion? It is just that, a fix. It offers a temporary high. It is a religion based on shame and guilt. The shame and guilt is like a coffee stain on the soul. The stain can only be removed by God. The only place one can find this particular God is in this particular church, and quite often with this particular preacher. The adherents of this religion are saved. Those who have not found their way to this religion are not. Those inside will be going to heaven. Those outside are headed for hell.

Quick-fix religions offer easy answers to life's most complex problems. All adherents must have the same beliefs—what I call spiritual cloning. The Bible is worshipped. It is a road map to the perfect life. There is no room for interpretation. The Holy Spirit was finished inspiring once the Good Book was written. The Old Testament is only there as background to the New Testament.

Quick-fix religions make "the end" the hope. Little time or energy is spent dealing with building the Kingdom on this earth. Here, the preaching and teaching is about getting into heaven. We don't bring heaven to earth. We spend our lives making sure we will get there when we die. Heaven becomes the prize. Heaven is the reward for having had the right faith. Heaven is an exclusive club, and only those properly credentialed will get in.

Quick-fix religions are all about evangelizing. They want converts. Jesus is marketed like a product. Worship becomes an entertaining extravaganza. The choirs seem professional. The preachers all sound and look the same. The messages hammer at the same two or three nails—how to go to heaven, who is going to heaven, and why the others are not going to heaven.

So what is wrong with that? If someone finds faith in a quick-fix religion, more power to him. To each his or her own. Right? No, I boldly disagree. Quick-fix religions offer the cheapest possible grace—grace without discipleship, grace without building the Kingdom, grace without a celebration of diversity. Cheap grace tries to look like genuine grace, but it gives itself away by sounding judgmental and self-righteous.

Quick-fix religions ultimately destroy spirituality and prevent maturation. Spirituality and maturation are fueled by questions. Doubts spark growth and change. Quick-fix religion sees life in either/or terms. Mature spirituality sees it from a both/and perspective. Quick-fix religions see faith as either you have it or you don't. Mature spirituality sees faith as original blessing—we all have it. Quick-fix religion sees heaven as private property. Mature spirituality recognizes heaven as a reality over which we have no control.

Mature spirituality encourages questioning. Mature spirituality celebrates diversity. Mature spirituality claims no special rank or privilege. Mature spirituality has no hierarchy. Mature spirituality is not for sale. Mature spirituality does not offer a momentary high, but rather a long walk of peace and justice upon this good earth. Mature spirituality is not focused on the great beyond, but on the here and now. Mature spirituality never claims to own God, only to be in close contact.

Looking to the Skies

The earth sways beneath our feet. Our knees quake. Our hearts shudder. We look to the skies. Maybe the answer is up there. As a people in desperate need of uplifting, we gaze upward. We hope that the solution is written in the stars. Maybe aliens will provide us the vital clues. Could it be that angels will nudge us along the proper path? Does the man in the moon hold the secret?

To some degree I believe in all of the above. Astrology, aliens, angels—they are all worthy of our interest and wonder. What I question is the spiritual value of wealthy Americans looking to the skies for answers and avoiding the issues we face on this earth. I believe a chat with a person who is sick or homeless or in prison, is of greater spiritual value than a conversation with an angel. I believe building a house for Habitat for Humanity is more deeply spiritual than spending a thousand bucks on a weekend to learn how to meditate.

I simply reject the Americanization of spirituality. Spirituality should not yield profits. It should not make gurus wealthy. It should not be accessible and affordable only for the wealthy. Mature spirituality is priceless. The poor have the greatest spirituality to dispense. Spirituality is found at the bottom.

The Questions
How can I bring heaven to earth today? Will I? Why or why not?

The Prayer
O God, let us save our precious planet. Let us make this globe our spiritual home. Let us bring heaven to the here and now. Let us cherish every morsel of your creation. Let us lift up our neighbor to partake in the banquet that is life. Amen.

Coming Down to Earth

What was most significant about the lunar voyage was not that men set foot on the moon but that they set eye on the earth.

—*Norman Cousins*

I have found a sure way to bring my faith into focus—a means of being spiritual, a method of renewing my spiritual energy, as close as I have ever come to a maturational guarantee: my camera.

Most mornings I go for a walk and take photos. I think of it as chasing beauty. I open my eyes wide. I look up and down and all around. I am aware of the potential for hidden beauty or the shock of awe. I regularly look through the lens. I focus. I see in the tiny square a glimpse of Creation. I notice the angle of the light. I pay attention to the movement of shadows. I am struck by my camera's ability to shout, "Now!"

It is spring. The sky is neon blue. The trees are lime. There are splashes of pink and white and lavender. The yellows are sadly fading, having done their job of heralding spring's arrival. The whole earth shimmers, as does the sea that surrounds Shelter Island. The beauty today is huge. It takes my breath away by its depth and size. Everywhere I look the camera says "Yes!" Selecting just a few shots will be like picking out penny candy when I was a kid.

I am struck by my good fortune. I live in a place where beauty blooms incessantly. So many scenes have an aura of eternity. Each photo plants a seed of faith. Beauty defies me not to believe. Beauty shouts of a Creator, an artist of classic skill. Beauty beckons us to its breast, to be held in awe by wonder.

Where must I go to find faith? To nature. To be in touch with the handiwork of God. To witness God's signature upon a season. To watch the earth dance in moonlight or under the tickling fingers of a spring rain. To be dazzled by the mystery of a star-splattered night or the infinite efforts of a civilization of ants. Under a microscope or telescope, the world dazzles us with its wonders.

The Natural

I love teenagers. Working with youth is one wild ride. I especially enjoy their lingo, the little catch phrases that dot their dialog. Their lingo is often prophetic, revealing a message that targets adults. As someone who works with youths, I pay attention to these messages. I hear it as spiritual slang. I know it is a language that will tell me something important.

"Get real." "Get a life." "Bogus." For a time, these were the big three of my youth group. What were they saying? I think it was obvious. They were pointing out the artificiality of so much of our culture. They were exposing the phoniness of our image-bound world. They were staking a claim on genuine. I experienced these young people as truly wanting to know real thoughts, real feelings, and real beliefs, not only from one another, but from the adults who were supposedly their mentors.

Natural. Real. Genuine. We can tell if someone asks us how we are and is sincerely interested in the answer. We know who our true friends are. We know the folks who would be there in a crisis. We also know when we are being phony. We are aware when our motivations are manipulative. We are conscious of our desire to impress.

Our culture brags that image is everything. We are told that Coke is the real thing. We are encouraged to keep our real selves under wraps. Don't let them see you sweat! We hide our humanity as if it were a scar. We never talk politics or religion. We try not to shed a tear. We never air our dirty laundry in public. In a nutshell, we learn at an early age how to fake it.

Faith must be natural. It must feel real. It must relate intimately to our reality. It must bring out our best—the genuine self. Faith is where we celebrate being human. Faith talks easily of religion and politics. Faith claims its tears. Faith shoulders its dirty laundry. Faith cleans that laundry with grace.

Earth Angels

I recently saw an elderly woman trip and fall in a department store parking lot. I ran to offer assistance. I was not alone. At least a dozen folks did the same. Three drivers slammed on their brakes, left their cars running, and scooted over to the gathering throng. The lady was cut badly and was quite shaken. An ambulance was called—stitches seemed warranted. The group worked in unison to calm her. As best we could, we attended to her every need.

Once the ambulance arrived, our gang backed off. Placed in a wheelchair, the woman waved at her caretakers and told us we were "her angels." We all waved back. We all assured her she would be fine. In a moment she was gone, and the crowd dispersed.

As I drove home, I thought about this gathering of angels. Earth angels. Good people being good neighbors. A cry for help and a rush to aid. I know we hear endless stories of human apathy and neglect, but I suspect that every day gangs of earth angels gather to offer a touch of grace to someone in need. Yet because it is good news, it will not make the news. It is, however, the real news of our planet. We are remarkably good people. Given the chance, we astound one another with our kindness. We care more than we contain.

Where can we look for faith? Does faith have a place where it tends to reside? Does faith grow best in certain soil?

We can look to nature to provide a daily spiritual spectacular. Nature is a moving picture of the heart of God. Nature tells us the story of God's endless love and infinite wisdom. Creation brings us home to the Creator.

We can look to human nature. We can look to our selves. When we are being true to our selves, the genuine article, we reflect God. We are created in God's image.

To be real is to be true to that image. God's image is no carnival mirror. It is an accurate depiction of the face of God.

We can look to one another. The earth is populated with angels. People of uncanny humor, courage, compassion, decency, and faith. People who make God proud. People who have no use for the fantasy lands of our culture. People who have come down to earth. People who live their faith on the ground, rooted in respect for reality. Real people living real lives. Earth angels. They're everywhere!

The Questions
When, where, and why am I fake? With whom am I most genuine? Why? What is it that I risk in being true to my self? What is the price I pay by being phony?

The Prayer
O God, let us see beauty. Let us witness the beauty of the earth, our selves, and our neighbors. May this beauty inspire us to believe. May we live as God's angels on this earth. May we knowingly choose to reflect God's image. Amen.

Coming to Our Senses

The truest expression of a people is in its dances and its music. Bodies never lie.

—Agnes DeMille

I had noticed the brief clip in one morning's *New York Times*. A meteor shower was scheduled for 5 A.M. I am not a morning person. I thought I had ruled it out, but around 4:45 A.M. I suddenly sat up in bed and made the decision to attend the event. I drove into Sag Harbor, got my 7-Eleven 20-ounce coffee, and took my place on the pier with about two dozen onlookers. Just after 5 the show began.

Slivers of light criss-crossed the sky. At times they grew bright enough to detect a leading ball. At one point the sky appeared to be quietly exploding. It was lovely. I was dumbstruck by this brief spectacle, speechless at the vastness of the universe. Nobody on the pier spoke. There was only a holy hush of *oohs* and *aahs*.

I felt a lump grow in my throat. I was conscious of its powerful but gentle presence. What did it mean? What is the lump made of? Who or what shapes the lump? Why a lump? Why now? What is the purpose of a lump in the throat? Is there a hidden message here?

I knew. I had no real epiphany or revelation, just an awareness. The lump in my throat told me of the presence of God. It was a sign, a symbol, a marker. The lump in my throat spoke to me of a reality whose beauty I could not grasp. The lump was filled with the grace of God. It was shaped and formed by faith. I beheld a meteor shower and washed myself in wonder.

A Body of Knowledge

Our bodies are miracles. The vast network of veins. The intricacies of muscles and joints working in harmony to create movement. The spectacular brain. The gifts of sight, sound, taste, touch, and smell. The mysterious power of healing. The uncanny sense of balance in all its systems. The body is a universe. The human body carries God's signature on every part.

The human body is also a factory of faith. The body is incessantly manufacturing messages from God. These messages tell us of our joy and happiness, our fear and dread, our weariness or loneliness. These messages are not written in any secret code. This is a language we all know. It is our native tongue. It is also, unfortunately, becoming a lost language. Like Latin, this spiritual dialect has gone out of fashion.

I get goose bumps when I hear Betty Buckley sing "Memories." I still get a shiver up and down my spine whenever I see a replay of the Twin Towers collapsing. I am moved to tears whenever Scrooge yells to the boy outside his window to go get the prize turkey. I find the smell of lilacs to be intoxicating. I want to jump for joy when I see kids sledding. I am in awe of how a symphony is composed, a computer works, or a human can stroll on the moon.

My body is speaking to me of goodness and beauty and love. It reminds me to stop and look and listen. My body begs me to take notice. At times I am being warned that I am out of balance, that I need rest or change or intimacy. If my body fails to get my attention, I get sick. Then I have to slow down and rest. Then I have nothing else to do but pay attention to my body.

Most of the time the body is trying to inform us that we are fine. There is no need to rush. There is no need to worry. There is no reason to be afraid. We need to stop running away from death. Every day we are living we are also dying. Don't push the river; it will flow all by itself.

Our bodies are effective communicators. The language they speak is clear and precise. It speaks volumes. We need to listen. What we will hear is the Word of God.

Common Sense

There is a little poem by Ogden Nash that I often use when I conduct weddings. It goes something like this, "To keep the love a brimmin' within the marriage cup, whenever you're wrong admit it, and whenever you're right, shut up!" I like this poem because it goes to what I believe is the central issue of marriage: A good marriage is all about common sense.

Common sense is knowing what we know. It is trusting our hearts. It is relying on our own innate wisdom. A good marriage is grounded in common sense—two people who know when they need to be together and when they must be apart. Two who know when to compromise or change. Two who understand when to speak or listen. Two people bonded by the ability to laugh at themselves. Two people who trust each other's word.

Just as we must learn to trust our bodies to keep us informed of God's wishes, so we must rely heavily on our common sense. God has planted myriad seeds of wisdom within us. Common sense is the garden of God's will. We know when we need to forgive or be forgiven. We know our longings and desires. We know when we are lying. We know what is phony or fake. We know the truth when we hear it. We know mercy when we see it. We even know what matters. We know what will last forever.

Common sense is just that—common. It is our divine inheritance. We are imprinted with God's wishes and will. We are originally blessed. We are innately wise. It is only when we start listening to the false promises of the world that we lose our common sense.

The world would have us believe that some people are born superior to others. The world teaches us that we are what we do, who we know, how we look, or what we wear. The world brainwashes us into believing that money makes all the difference and that power must be used to keep others in their place. The world is crazy enough to proclaim that living a lie is simply the price of success. The world places little stock in faith. Faith has no value on the open market.

Senseless

A suicide bomber. A young woman or man walks into a store or restaurant or village square. Around his waist he carries explosives. He blows himself up. Often many innocent people are also killed. The bomber leaves a note behind. He claims to be serving God. God's wrath and revenge is being expressed. An eye for an eye. This is a holy war.

Does this make any sense? Any *real* sense? Can we ever truly explain such insanity? Can we accept the validity of a faith that claims such a vile and violent God? Does such an explosion of hate have anything to say about God, except for God's glaring absence? What in heaven's name is a holy war?

Blind faith is senseless faith. It is faith gone numb. It is a faith deadened by rage and revenge. It is faith without thinking. It is faith in a one-sided God. Our side. My side. It is faith in a God we control like a puppet. Such a faith is bound to yield senseless acts of violence. It is a faith detached from the body, heart, mind, and soul. It is a faith without connections to any of our divine senses.

Blind faith simply chooses not to see. It wears blinders. It loses perspective. It fails to look at the other side. The human side. The side where mystery and miracles reside. The side they cannot control. Sadly, ironically, it is this side that would reveal to them what they ultimately seek—the face of God.

The Questions
What has my body taught me today? What consistently moves me to tears? Why? When do I feel most excited and energized? Why?

The Prayer
O God, teach us to respect the infinite majesty and mystery of our bodies. May we learn from this body of divine knowledge. May we listen attentively to the messages our bodies send. May we hear our bodies speak to us of the presence of God. Amen.

Wisdom's White Flag

Only a fool tests the depth of the water with both feet.

—*African proverb*

Dr. Kelt is my doctor and my friend. We've known each other for several years. I respect and trust him. I have no reason to fear him. I had, however, been unconsciously avoiding him. He pointed this out the minute I walked into his office. I looked puzzled. I got on the scale. I almost fainted. I had ballooned to 335 pounds. We both immediately knew the reason for my avoidance.

I have struggled with my weight my entire adult life. I have lost more than 80 pounds on eight different occasions. I have tried at least 10 different diets. All worked for a time, but the weight never stayed off. Soon the pounds would return, plus 10 or 15 more. I was the proverbial yo-yo dieter.

My wife recently died as a direct result of her obesity. She was in the midst of her second gastric bypass when surgical complications took her life. I had been her co-dependent eating partner for years, and following her death, my eating became a means of calming my wild grief.

For 20 years I have known I am a compulsive over-eater. I know my bad habits. I don't eat all day and reward myself all night. I seldom eat when hungry. I use food as a friend, even a sexual partner. Food is my one true indulgence. In a life devoted to being a semi-saint, food has become a means of declaring my humanity.

Three hundred thirty-five pounds. The number was frightening. What had I done? How could I have let things get this out of control? Didn't I care about my life? How could I put myself at such risk? How could I do this to my son, Justin? Would he watch two parents eat themselves to death? I was devastated by those numbers. I could feel my soul bouncing on a sharp, hard place. It was like falling on razor blades. I had hit bottom.

Surrendering

After the appointment I took a walk. I was suddenly aware that I had literally stopped exercising. As I walked, I wept. I was swept by a swarming shame. Being obese in America is horrid. I thought about how many things my weight was impacting. I no longer played tennis or basketball or baseball—sports I was good at and loved. I didn't attend high school or college reunions, and I would not contact old friends when I returned to my hometown for a visit. I slept all the time. I was frequently sick. I had become addicted to television. Except for my work, I lived in hiding.

I spoke out loud about all the health issues that were a direct result of my weight. My cholesterol and blood pressure were high. I had diabetes. I was prone to upper respiratory infections. I had stomach problems. My knees ached. My eyes were weakening. I sweated like a pig. I needed to take a handful of medications every morning and several more each night. Hazy fears of stroke or heart attack were constant.

My first reaction was to take control of the situation. I mentally crafted out the perfect diet and exercise regimen. I would be like the Nike ad—just do it! The fantasy of a swift ride to slender exploded. I was hopelessly out of control. My other efforts to control my weight had all failed. My spirits sagged as I realized I could never willpower my way to a healthy weight. It was my infamous willpower that had helped get me into this pickle. My perfectionism was the yo-yo's string.

I stopped. I was in so much pain I could barely breathe. I prayed. For the very first time I admitted to myself that only God could restore me to sane eating. Though I had long ago admitted to myself that I was an addict, I had never before truly turned it over to God.

Funny. I am a minister. One would think that God would be the first place I would turn. Not really. We all have that one issue that brings us to our knees. This was mine. On my knees I would learn three essential truths about myself and my weight: first, that I am not God; second, that I can only control whether or not I let God in; third, that until I quit trying to take on the weight of the world, I will be obese.

It is too early to tell if I will lose the weight. It will be a long and hard fight. Trusting God is my sole battle plan. At this point the only thing I can honestly say is that I have waved the white flag for the very first time.

Knee Knowledge

When we are on our knees, we know we are not God. On our knees we accept the limits of our humanity. We recognize that we are not in control of anything. We are not in charge. All our certainty is illusion. From our knees we can see that life does not come with warranties or guarantees.

Initially, knee knowledge is frightening. We feel diminished, inconsequential. Being on our knees is a posture of humility. On our knees, our arrogance is shown to be ignorance, our grandiosity proves foolish, and any boasting sounds silly. It is from our knees that we do our best and most fervent praying.

Knee knowledge soon transforms fear into faith. We learn of the freedom to be found in surrender. No longer trying to make a name for ourselves or proving to the world we are a somebody, we can relax and be ourselves. Life is no longer about piling up accomplishments and achievements. Life is an exercise in receiving. Life is a pure gift.

Do you have a tough time receiving a gift, especially one given spontaneously, for no other reason than to express affection? I think we all do. This is sad. The day is such a gift, a gracious gift from a loving God who adores us. God does not ask us to squeeze the value out of the day. God does not call on us to wring the day dry of its worth. God asks only that we receive the gift and open it.

To open a day is to enter it like a sponge. Faith opens the heart and mind and soul to let in the Word of God. The Word of God is life itself. Life, like a drop of water, cannot be grasped. Life can only be absorbed.

Follow the Leader

We tend to be lousy receivers. We are equally bad followers. Again, we live in a culture that values leaders. We all want to be boss. Following is for losers. Following is for the lazy. Following is the result of a lack of ambition or talent or both.

Faith is following. Faith is knowing that we need a leader. Faith is looking to God. Faith is trusting God to know where we are headed. Faith is being confident that God will show us the way to the Promised Land—the Kingdom on this earth. Faith is a journey home to God.

Faith is full of wisdom—the wisdom to recognize the bottom when we hit it; to wave the white flag when we are out of control; to accept that when we are at wit's end, God's wits are still about him/her; to understand that our most significant action is receiving; to believe that all true spiritual movement is following.

The primary source of wisdom is prayer. Praying is any and all effort to connect with a higher power. It may be speaking, sighing, or staring. Conscious or unconscious. Active or passive. Prayer is the tool we use to open up. Once we are open, we are free to attend the banquet—the glorious life God has set before us.

A Follow-Up Exam

I am convinced that my weight and health are both issues of faith. I will need to learn how to nourish myself with life. I need to be full of and on God. God must set the menu. God alone can teach me how to have a balanced diet and life. God will expect discipline. God will require my undivided attention. God is never a magic wand solution.

The Questions
When was the last time I was spiritually on my knees?
What did I learn there? When was the last time I chose to
follow? Where did it take me?

The Prayer
O God, without you I am nothing. With you … I am all I
can dream. Grant me the strength to fall into your arms.
Amen.

Loosen Up, Lighten Up

*How we spend our days is, of course,
how we spend our lives.*

—Annie Dillard (The Writing Life)

A bad day.

I get up out of bed but long only to return. My sleep was agitated. All the worries of the day before are still present. My fear is robust. My anxiety is swollen. I cannot figure out what I am doing or why. I feel inept. I am lonely. Lost.

As the day wears on, my body grows taut. My mind aches. My heart feels battered and bruised. My soul has formed cobwebs. Like falling dominos, I review my life's betrayals and defeats. I chronicle my losses. I douse myself in bad news. The tension thickens.

A bad day knows no dawn. There is little light. It is a drab darkness. Dull as February. Like sleet. Like muddy watercolors. There is no life to it. No vibrancy. No perspective. No faith. I wander aimlessly.

I am convinced that our world creates bad days. Our culture creates chaos. We are trapped in a way of life that grabs us by the throat and squeezes out the lifeblood. We are too busy. Stress swarms like mosquitoes. The ladder of success is way too high, as is the cost of climbing. We are alone too much. We are dead tired too often.

Think of how we speak of time. We buy time. Kill time. Spend time. Carve out time. We treat time, like the day, as our enemy. We seek to conquer that which God has given us for free. With the day as our opponent, no wonder we have so many bad days. Life was never meant to be a battle, let alone a war.

Loosen Up

We lead crazy lives, trying to juggle a hundred balls in the air, trying to keep everyone happy, trying to be perfect. We dig holes for ourselves. We get stuck in the mud of our own making. We choose stress, and that stress snaps our spirit. We grow rigid. We lose flexibility. Muscles wither. Now we are not only stuck, we lack the strength to climb out of the pit.

Think of life as a marathon. Not only must we be in good spiritual shape, but we must also be loose for the race. How do we get loose? We need to stretch our minds and imaginations. We must bend our will into conformity with God's. We must shake out the prejudice and hate. We must exercise our love. We must flex our forgiveness. We must reach out a hand to others. We must breathe the air of faith deep into our lungs. Then we are ready to run.

A Negative

The more uptight we become, the darker our world becomes. Light cannot penetrate the walls of worry. We are like black holes. Our light has imploded. It cannot be seen. It is still there, but visible only to the eye of God.

As the light fades, we become more negative. We get harsher, mean, and at times, downright cruel. Our love has been drained. Our hope has disappeared. We blame others for our misfortunes. We find scapegoats for our problems. We find fault.

Faith is light. It is to be spiritually enlightened. The more uptight and negative we become, the more our faith retreats into the shadows. It is like watching an eclipse. We can see the aura of light, but at the center is pure blackness. Our mood grows dark. Our dreams dim. God flickers like a light bulb in an electrical storm.

A photo negative shows us where there is light and the absence of light. All photography is about light. We are actually taking pictures of light. A pure black negative is a picture that did not turn out. It is worthless. It has nothing to say or show. We would not waste time processing a black/blank negative.

So it is with us. So it is with our culture. The more negative we become, the more we become a waste of space. We have become a nation of cynics. We know the price of everything but value nothing. Our television screens celebrate finding the weakest link, mudslinging debates, sarcastic and arrogant judges, scorned lovers, and exiled survivors. Civility has all but vanished. We are a people who have put on the gloves.

It only takes one cloud to block out the sun. Sadly, we live in a culture that encourages us to become that cloud.

Lighten Up

Think of life as a painting. Imagine painting in the dark. Think of trying to paint a black hole. Both are difficult. Both are doomed to produce poor results. Both will yield little to no satisfaction. Light is a fundamental requirement of all great art, including the art of living.

What does it mean to lighten up? I believe that it means we need to take our importance less seriously and our living more so. I believe it means to stop obsessing about that which does not matter, and to strive to locate that which does. I think it is worrying less about how *long* we will live and more about *how* we live.

Lightening up is the relinquishment of worry and stress. It is letting go. It is genuinely letting God take over. It is taking the baggage of our backgrounds and placing it on God's shoulders. It is letting God lift the burdens off our backs. It is walking in the bright light of a good day.

The Questions
What makes me uptight? What relaxes me? What do I keep in the dark? About what am I in denial?

The Prayer
O God, let me relax. Let me take time to re-create. Loosen me up. Stretch my soul. Flex my faith. Let me run the race with no worry about winning. O God, let me walk in the light. Keep my eyes open. Let me be aware of your presence. Let me bask in the warm glow of your love. Let me see with your eyes. Let me envision your Kingdom. Amen.

Homing Devices

*The home is not the one tame place in the
world of adventure. It is the one wild place in
the world of rules and set tasks.*

—*G. K. Chesterton*

Faith is a journey. The destination is always the same—
home. A place where we are at ease. The experience of
belonging. A sense of deep-rooted safety and security.
Being known and understood and accepted. A dwelling
where one feels cherished and adored.

As children, that place is where our family lives. It is
there that we know the rules and the roles and rituals.
We know the menu by heart. We know the bathroom
sounds and the kitchen smells. We know which blanket
and pillow are ours. When the door closes, the world is
left behind—the boogeyman has no key.

Our families are where we learn about grace. Within
the walls of our homes we hear messages of unconditional love and praise dominates. At home we know the

sweet sound of forgiveness and that every cry for help will be quickly answered.

As we have all come to learn, we are all from dysfunctional families. Yes, many of us come from warm, caring, tender-loving families. Many of us come from cold, awkward, stiff-upper-lipped families. Still others of us come from families and homes that resembled a demolition derby. We would be lucky to come out a wreck.

As life progresses, we mature. Maturation yields wisdom. Wisdom would tell us that the unconditional love we seek cannot come in human form. Our parents, mates, children, friends, mentors, or family may do their best to blanket us with grace, but they will always fall short. Grace can ultimately only be offered to us by God. The true home we seek is with our God.

The longing for home is not for a hometown or a house jammed with memories. It is to be held in the embrace of an adoring God.

Asking for Directions

I am a typical male. I don't ask for directions. I just get lost. Paradoxically, or logically, if taken from a faith perspective, being lost has always led me home—to God.

I am not encouraging you to get lost; I am simply acknowledging that it is impossible to live without getting lost. Getting lost is one of life's few guarantees. At some point we will lose our way. We will ask ourselves where we are going and why? We will question our direction and our destination. We will pull off to the side of the road, beat our fists against the dash, and scream.

What we need to scream is "HELP!" What we need to ask for is directions. One of the greatest of all homing devices is the act of asking for help. Homing devices are those attitudes or behaviors, rites or rituals, or positions or perspectives that enable us to find our way home. A homing device is something that reminds us that we know the way. A homing device is a good map.

Asking for help is such a map. Asking for help admits our humanness. When we claim to be human, we have stopped trying to play God. We have accepted that we are not in control. We are free to let God come in. Once in the door, God can show us the way.

God does not offer us a detailed road map. This is not that kind of map. God points in a direction. God points us back to living and loving and learning.

God asks us to get back into the middle of our lives. God calls for a return to reality, only this time the reality will be faced in faith. God wants to show us how to have our future shaped and defined by our faith.

God will also show us where to stop and stay, what the meaningful historical sights are, and where the beautiful scenic overlooks are. God wants the journey to be pleasant and enjoyable. God will also warn us of the dangers and detours on the road. Most of all, God will encourage us to take back roads, to stay off the expressways, where we miss everything. Life is meant to be a long, winding road through pretty country.

Destination

Where are we headed? Our world does not seem to know. Worse yet, we don't seem to care. What we do know is that we spend a lot of time wanting to get away. We long to go someplace where we can forget about life for a while. We yearn for an escape.

Faith knows exactly where it is headed. Faith is about caring about that place. The place is the Kingdom. The manager is God. There is plenty of room.

Faith does not, however, offer escape. Coming home to God is also coming home to duty. Faith claims loving as a duty. Forgiveness. Mercy. Compassion. Community. The celebration of diversity. In God's house everyone has chores, and there are no excuses. Discipline is firm but fair.

Faith is the ultimate homing device. Prayer. Worship. Service. Sacrifice. Stewardship. Rites of passage. Rituals of bonding. All aspects of living faith aim at bringing us home to God. On this map all roads lead in one direction and to one place.

Homing Devices

Each year I discover new "homing devices." These are activities, attitudes, or actions that promote a connectedness to my Higher Power. This year I found the following to lead me home to God:

- Flying kites
- Watching butterflies
- Beginning each day by writing a thank you card to someone
- Making a big deal of a birthday

- Skipping
- Filling the sanctuary at our church with lilacs
- Literally forbidding myself to spend a second worrying
- Asking teenagers what gives them hope
- Asking adults where they have found their hope
- Learning to eat slowly—savoring each bite

Homing devices bring us back to what matters. They return us to our priorities. They root us in our faith.

The Questions
What homing devices work for me? What homing devices would I like to try? What would it be like to spend a day living at home with God?

The Prayer
O God, lead me home. Let me know that my journey needs to end in your embrace. Enable my feet to follow my heart's lead. Let me carve a daily path to a place of genuine security and hope. Amen.

The Gray Light of Grace

I would rather live in a world where my life is surrounded by mystery than live in a world so small that my mind could comprehend it.

—Harry Emerson Fosdick

I love to paint with watercolors. A tube of good watercolor is expensive. One small tube of Windsor Blue can go as high as $15. I am not rich, so I watch my pennies. I recently noticed that the colors I kept replacing were all hues of brown and blue. The greens were running low but had lasted for months. My reds and oranges seemed to last forever. Black and white showed no sign of use.

What struck me was the recognition that all grays are made by mixing blues and browns. My landscapes, even portraits, were primarily painted in shades of gray. The splash of bright color was just that, a splash. Most of the paper was covered in washes of various grays. It is gray that is the color of shadow.

Our lives are also painted in gray. Gray is the dominant mood and theme of living. This is not to say that life is dull or dreary. Gray can be as bright as ice and as dense as fog. Gray offers contrast to sunlight. Gray is what sets off the Light of God. Gray digs depth. Our lives are matted in gray.

Black and White Answers

In living color. Life is indeed lived in color—all the colors of the rainbow, the full spectrum of shades and hues. Life is not painted in blacks and whites. It is not paint-by-numbers. It is not a coloring book. There are no lines to confine us. There are no markings to tell us what or where the color should go. There is simply the sheet of paper, the paints, the brushes, and a God who calls us to paint.

A living faith does not have black and white answers. Black and white answers become law. The law becomes a means by which we judge others. Our judgments lead to prejudice. Our prejudice leads to hate. Our hate leads to violence. Ultimately, the law drains life of love and justice.

A living faith does not worship a book—even if it is the Good Book. Life cannot be contained by a book.

Life is not meant to be explained or defended. Life is to be received—lived. We worship a God who is alive and well, at work in our world and in our lives. We look to these pages, life being lived, to discover our truths.

A living faith holds that there is no single truth. There is not a one-size-fits-all faith. Faith is as diverse as the Creation. Faith comes in all shapes, sizes, and styles. Faith can be conservative or outrageous. It can be neatly tailored or floppy and layered. Faith expresses style. Our life styles are a matter of faith.

Paradox and Ambiguity

A living faith resides in paradox. A living faith is at home in ambiguity. A living faith understands that we are both human and divine, free to be slaves, full of doubt.

A living faith can embrace the strange ambiguity of spiritual truth. My Christian faith is built upon such seemingly incongruous values. The first will be last. The lost, found. Those that mourn will be blessed, as will the meek and the peacemaker.

The parables, Christ's teaching method, were packed with paradoxes. The worker who toils five minutes gets the same wages as the one who works all day. The father throws a big party for the son who went off and squandered his fortune, but hosts no such event for the older brother who stayed at home and worked his butt off. The penny offered by a poor widow is of far greater value than the big check offered by a rich man. All of Christ's lessons, like life itself, are encased in mystery.

A living faith knows it does not know the whole truth. The whole truth cannot be put into words. The whole truth comes only in glances and glimpses. We get a slice, not the whole cake. Even if it were served up to us on a silver platter, we could not eat it all. It is too much to swallow. It is too much spiritual food for a one-lifetime seating.

Mystery

A living faith loves a good mystery. Faith does not seek to unravel the mystery, but to follow it. The mystery will unravel itself. We need only watch for clues. We need to keep our eyes glued on the plot. We must be good listeners. We must pay attention to the twists and turns and notice the unsuspecting characters.

The truth of a good mystery is never found in the most likely spot. It is hidden—hidden out in the open, right under our noses, right before our eyes. It was there all the time.

A good detective is one who knows where to look, where not to look, and what hunches to play. He trusts his instincts. He follows all leads. He remains committed to the case.

A living faith will put one good mystery down, only to pick up another. The mystery must keep expanding. The plot grows thicker. The characters, more quirky. The story, more suspenseful. This is what keeps the reader glued to the pages. This is what keeps us endlessly enthralled with life.

The Color of Grace

Grace is the unconditional love of God. It is available to all. It is present in all things. It is everywhere. It is life's background noise. It is the gray wash onto which we dab our favorite bright colors.

Grace is gray. It is mysterious as fog, elusive as a cloud, shimmers like ice, and glistens like rain. It is a color that appears to hold no hue, yet is the one color that gives all other colors their shine.

Grace is in the background, working behind the scenes. Grace has no need for center stage, no need to get the good review. Grace is just doing its job, putting us in the right makeup or costume, creating the perfect set to make our acting believable, and making sure the spotlight is on us.

The Questions
Do I hold any black and white answers? Can I live with ambiguity? Can I enjoy the mystery? Can I add to the mystery?

The Prayer
O God, may I avoid all simple answers. May I reject black and white answers that declare human superiority and judgment. Make me comfortable with paradox. Encourage me to expand the mystery. Let me paint my life in vivid colors, dabbed onto a background awash in the gray light of God's Grace. Amen.

Living with Diversity

*If we cannot now end our differences, at least
we can help make the world safe for diversity.*

—John F. Kennedy

Creation. A bold statement of the Word of God. An explosion of raw beauty. Swirling chaos calms into miracle. Mystery finds a suitable home. Life is born.

All of Creation is emblazoned with God's signature. All reveals the nature of God's love. All displays the imagination of the Divine.

The hallmark of God's Creation is diversity—different sizes, shapes, and colors; myriad moods, tones, and textures; countless points and purposes; endless rhymes and reasons.

Human beings are Creation's high mark. We were created in the image of God, our minds jammed with thoughts and memories, our hearts heaped full of feelings and longings, our souls speaking languages as diverse as native tongues. Human beings—what a world of difference.

Why then, would God the Creator choose to create one solitary faith, one way of believing, one lone way of experiencing God, one isolated means of expressing faith? Does that make sense? How can we reconcile the notion of one faith with the vast diversity of Creation? When it came time to create faith, did God suddenly change course?

A living faith is a diverse faith. When faith is alive, it flows in many directions. Revelations and epiphanies are as many as the planets and stars. No two are alike. Each of us contains a unique experience of the Presence of God. Each faith is of equal value. Each faith is a declaration of human inspiration and divine imprint.

A living faith has no interest in competing with another faith. There may be fascination in comparing, but not for reason of judgment. A living faith cannot be ranked. There is no hierarchy. A living faith can never be cloned. A living faith is as unique as the life being lived. A living faith cannot be confined or defined by a creed. It is never bound or gagged by protocol. It cannot be tamed.

The Holy Spirit

Early in her career, my late wife was often questioned about the validity of her ordination. The Bible was waved before her as proof positive there were no female disciples. I would get infuriated. Chris remained calm. She would simply say, "If I am not called to the ministry, then the Holy Spirit is a liar." Chris drew the bottom line. No book, not even the Bible, could be used to corral the Holy Spirit.

The Holy Spirit is free. It can and will move wherever it wishes. We cannot control these movements anymore than we can chew our own teeth. The Holy Spirit will not be told who is acceptable or worthy of being touched. The transforming powers of the Holy Spirit are available to all. We do not make the choice. Our words do not control the actions of the Spirit. God chooses us. God's Word informs and illumines us.

The Holy Spirit is inclusive. God's Spirit reaches out to us all. God's embrace is for everyone. Our role is to receive that holy hug. We are only in charge of receptivity. There is no prejudice in the Holy Spirit other than an attraction to an open mind, heart, and soul.

The Holy Spirit is not moved by public opinion, the whim of popularity, or the results of polling. The Holy Spirit is the flow of grace. It is the movement of faith. The Holy Spirit consistently travels down the road less traveled. It regularly lifts up the least of these to be our spiritual mentors and guides. The world does not hold the reins on the Holy Spirit. The Holy Spirit reigns over the world.

The Holy Spirit is not owned by one religion. It is not under human control. We do not determine who is called or to what they are called. We either trust God or we don't. God is in charge.

Celebrate Does Not Mean Tolerate

I am a Christian. I believe in Jesus Christ. Jesus had 12 disciples. He chose them. I suspect he chose some women, too, but I will leave that for another book. He chose 12 men who could not agree on a thing, who had different backgrounds and histories, different customs and callings, and different religious perspectives. Each was unique. These 12 would form a community, a spiritual family. They were the friends and colleagues of Jesus.

Why would Jesus choose 12 with so little in common? Why create a spiritual family with such potential for conflict? Didn't Christ set the disciples up to be a ministry in chaos?

I believe Jesus saw diversity as the essence of creativity. Diversity demands consensus building. Diversity requires respect. Diversity necessitates love. These 12 were called to a ministry. The ministry was one of mercy. They were to be mercy makers. If they failed to show one another love and respect, their ministry would fail. It was their calling to this ministry that held them together.

Celebrating diversity is not about tolerating one another. It is not allowing someone to disagree. It is listening intently to their point of view. It is not acknowledging the validity of their faith. It is wanting to learn more about it. It is not pointing out the difference and saying it's okay. It is highlighting the difference as a source of joy.

Celebrating diversity is learning to enjoy difference, to revel in variety, to thrive on assortment, to know that life is a medley of miracles. We are life's mixed nuts.

Heaven

I have had three recent revelations concerning heaven.

First, at my wife's funeral, I made the comment that I imagined her now enjoying the same diversity of friendship she had savored on earth—male and female, Christian and Jew, gay and straight. People of faith. People of doubt. Sinners and saints.

Second, I showed Steven Spielberg's brilliant film *Schindler's List* to my youth group. I was asked by one of the youth if these Jews went to heaven. I was dumbstruck by the thought of the Nazi Christians claiming heaven, while the smoke of Auschwitz ovens descended to hell.

Third, when the Twin Towers of the World Trade Center came crashing down, I was acutely aware of the diversity of human life and faith the buildings contained. Did only the Christians go to heaven? What a repugnant thought.

Heaven has a wide door and an even wider mercy. It is mercy magnified. Heaven is under God's management. I suspect there is always room, and room for all. God's door is always open. It is only a human who might slam a door in someone's face. God remains the perfect host, waiting patiently for guests to arrive. We have all received our invitation.

Look at our world today. Wars of religion. Terrorist fanatics. Widening divisions. Prejudice rising. Walls of hate being erected. People claiming to own God. People claiming to have the only truth. People bashing the beliefs of their neighbors.

Imagine a world where diversity was celebrated. Imagine a civilization of mature civility, a gathering of nations that respected and enjoyed difference. A true melting pot. What a difference, what a world of difference. A truly diverse world would make all the difference in the world.

The Questions

Am I prejudiced? Do I discriminate against others? How? Why? Am I afraid of difference? How am I learning to accept and enjoy difference?

The Prayer

O God, enable me to embrace the diversity of your creation. Let me find joy in difference. Create a clean heart in me. Erase my prejudice. Wipe away my need to discriminate. Let me write my story with a love for all peoples and languages. Let me speak the spiritual language of mercy. Let my name be Grace. Amen.

Living the Questions

*A sudden, bold, and unexpected question doth
many times surprise a man and lay him open.*

—Francis Bacon

A living faith seeks the genuine good life. This good life
seeks goodness. Goodness is not found in what we do
for a living. Goodness is centered in our being. We can
be good. A living faith is all about being good.

One way to be good is to ask good questions. A good
question addresses subjects that matter. It is coated in
mystery. It has a seed of miracle at the core. It is a catalyst to thought. It makes us feel. It inspires belief. A
good question digs deep. It is never shallow. It goes to
the heart of the issue—being alive.

A living faith asks good questions on a daily basis.
Asking good questions is an act of faith. It is a means of
devotion. It is a central task of the spiritual life. Good
questions force us to mature. True maturity is growth

aimed directly at God. By living these questions, we establish an intimacy with God.

Asking Questions

As a minister, I do a good deal of marriage counseling. I am frequently struck by how little some couples communicate. Talk is reduced to checking in, touching base, or reviewing a calendar. Conversation is conducted on the surface. The topics are kept mundane. Many marriages avoid intimate conversation as a means of staying safe. A marriage may be safe and still die.

I work with couples, helping them ask one another good questions—questions that express a desire to know and understand, questions that show a respect for intelligence and feelings, questions that probe for the soul. Once a good question is asked, it is hard to turn back. It demands a response. The response demands to be heard. The exchange demands to be taken seriously. Serious conversation is what is lacking in many failing marriages.

Couples who begin to talk seriously with one another soon realize that "serious" does not mean "depressing." Just the opposite. A good talk is exhilarating. It is a release. It is a gust of fresh air.

When couples ask one another good questions, they are renewing their vows. They are saying they are still interested in each other. They are speaking a language of admiration and respect. They are telling their partner that they matter. When we want to know what a person thinks, it is because we value them. We value their history, perspective, and insight.

A good marriage knows that a good question is never fully answered. Good marriages expect change. A change of mind is seen as a sign of maturity, not as being flighty. A change of heart is found to be invigorating, not troubling. A good marriage keeps the love alive by asking living questions, questions alive with interest and intelligence and full of spunk and spirit.

Pray Without Ceasing

A life of faith is a prayer; a living prayer. Our lives express our prayers. Our prayers give voice to our faith. God hears our prayers by witnessing our lives.

A living faith prays without ceasing. Prayer is listening to the questions asked by God. Prayer is asking God all of our questions. Prayer is the establishment of an intimate relationship with God.

Prayer does not seek out answers. Prayer seeks out God. All prayer is rooted in questioning. All prayer is at base a quest for understanding the will of God. All prayer carries the wish for an answer and the understanding that no answer will yield complete satisfaction.

A living faith is alive with prayer. Daily we come to God in search of answers, and daily God sends us back to our lives. God points the way but will not hold our hand. God trusts us to find our own way. God respects our instinct to find our way home. Our home is in the midst of life.

How do I pray? Ask a good question. Be awake and alert, aware and conscious, open and receptive. Then wait. The answer will come. It will come as another good question. Each question digs deeper. Each question will get closer to the treasure buried beneath the surface.

Intimacy

A living faith lives the questions. It is alive with the quest for truth. Good questions seek intimacy on all levels.

Living the questions means we are on intimate terms with ourselves. We know our innards. We know the terrain of our soul. We have paid frequent visits to our heart. We enjoy wandering about our mind.

We have spent ample time getting to know ourselves. If we are asked what we think, we can articulate a response. If we are asked what we are feeling, we quickly retrieve an answer. If we are asked to speak about our faith, we state our convictions.

Living the questions frees us to love our neighbor. If we care enough to ask good questions, we are genuinely interested in our neighbor's well-being. Love is not so much the answer, as it is a question that expresses care, concern, and compassion. Love seeks to open up the one we love. A good question is a means of prying open the heart. A living question knocks at the door of the soul and waits to be invited in.

Living the questions establishes intimate contact with God. The good questions of our prayers create meaningful contact with our Creator. When we address life's biggest questions, we let God know of our devotion and respect. We want to know God's will. We want to feel God's pain. We want to share God's joy. We want to be co-Creators. A living faith is not a monologue. It is a dialog with an adoring partner.

When was the last time someone asked you a good question? How did it make you feel? I bet it made you feel loved. I am confident it was received as an expression of genuine care. Being asked a good question feels good. It also encourages us to be good. When we are loved, the good within us yearns for release.

Love is mutual. It is a reciprocal trade agreement. A good question aims not for an answer, but to express love. The answer is the response to this love. How do we respond to being loved? We act loveable. We become better people. We love. What goes around comes around. The living question has come full circle. It is this circle that contains the answer. The circle holds only love.

The Questions
What questions make me feel most alive? What questions inspire me to grow and mature? What questions require intimacy for me to share?

The Prayer

O God, make me alive with questions. Contact me with your questions. Connect me intimately with life's big questions so that I may hear the ceaseless buzz of life being lived to the fullest. May my questions be full. Amen.

Living Our Longings

Ideals are like the stars. We never reach them but, like the mariners on the sea, we chart our course by them.

—Carl Schurz

The desire for a cold glass of water after a long hike on a hot day. The need to be held after we receive bad news. The hope to be remembered long after we are gone. Longings are our passions. Our deepest desires. Our wishes. Our hopes. They are what move us, and animate our being.

We have physical longings—hunger, thirst, clothing for warmth, shelter for protection from the elements, lust, sleep, bodily functions. If these longings are not addressed, we are in pain. Our bodies suffer. We may die.

We have emotional longings—the desire to be known and understood, the need to be heard and respected, the appetite for friendship, the hunger for love, the craving for family and home. If these longings are not met, we grow sad. This sadness may deepen to depression. Despair can consume the human heart and leave it broken.

We have spiritual longings—the thirst for knowledge, the yearning for a sense of meaning and worth, the hope for a genuine purpose. We want to make a difference. We wish to leave our mark on life. We hunger for holiness. We covet faith. If we fail to pay attention to these longings, our soul will wither and rot. Our spirits will decay. We will lose hope and faith. We cannot love.

We live in a world that is terrified of claiming spiritual longings. This is uncharted territory. There are no maps. There are few good guides. The world often encourages us to play it safe and stay at home, choose security and stability. Why rock the boat? Why climb life's tallest spiritual peaks? We should just be content with life in the valley.

A living faith strives to satisfy our spiritual longings. It will risk wandering in the wilderness. It is possessed of a courage that will drive it to freedom. A living faith is not interested in playing it safe. It is interested in coming alive, living life to the fullest, stretching the boundaries, making the sky the limit, rocking the boat. And why not? We know how to swim. More than anything, a living faith wants a peak experience.

A living faith is unafraid. Fear dictates that we expect the worst. We wait for the bomb to drop. We live as though there were no tomorrow. A living faith expects the best. It drops the bombshells. It creates a better tomorrow. A living faith is free from fear, free to dive into the middle of life, free to believe that life is an ocean of grace in which we cannot drown.

Dying To

Have you ever asked yourself, "What am I dying to do? To be?" You may be stunned to hear your answers. Often, what we are dying for is quite simple—time with friends, time to play, a chance to travel or explore an area of interest, picking up a good book or an old hobby, taking a hike, listening to our favorite music, writing a letter, cooking a great meal, cleaning a closet, or perhaps doing nothing for an entire day.

What we are dying to do and be is almost always of a spiritual nature. We are dying to nourish our souls. We long to feed our spirits. Our spiritual self is hungering for time spent with God, looking for glances and glimpses of grace, and thirsting for a drink from an ever-flowing stream. We may literally be dying from failing to offer the soul food and drink.

I am dying to make more money. I am dying to own more stuff. I am dying to have more time to work. Can you imagine giving such an answer? No! It would sound absurd. We would find it silly. It would make us laugh. The real joke is that so many of us live those exact answers. We starve our souls. We pay no attention to our spiritual appetites. We offer ourselves a spiritual menu with only desserts.

Living Life to the Fullest

The youthful spirit has been severely tempered, dampened, and is on the verge of being extinguished.

Today's youth play it safe. They want to learn if it has relevance. Relevance means it makes money. They want to know what is in it for them. They want job security. They want to know that they can buy what they want, when they want. They want financial freedom. They want it all now. If they cannot afford it, they want it on credit. They live as if there indeed was no tomorrow.

I experience today's youth as having narrow objectives and slim hopes. These are not passionate kids. They show little desire to set the world on fire. They are neither idealists nor rebels. They are practical. They are practically lifeless and spiritually dead. They like life when it is smooth, like a flat line on a heart monitor.

I know I am generalizing. Not all youth are in a spiritual coma. But I think I am correct when I say that what God means by an abundant life is not what our young have in mind. We have not been good spiritual mentors. We have not faced up to our responsibility to speak to spiritual longings. We have failed to make a pitch for spiritual satisfaction. We didn't risk pontificating on the difference between the pursuit of happiness and the shock of joy. We did not deliver the needed sermon on living life to the fullest—not filling up our lives with stuff we do not need.

Living our longings—the longing for happiness … balance … forgiveness … home … hope … joy … meaning … eternity … God. These longings are the very pulse of life. Meeting these longings yields satisfaction, inner peace, and serenity. A life that does not speak to and of these longings is hollow, empty, and lacking in content and consequence. It is as dry as dust, as dull as a list.

A full life is one that is in daily dialog with these longings. Longings speak the language of faith—faith in a living God, faith in life itself, faith that witnesses not with words but by living.

A living faith fills itself on the energy and excitement aroused by longings. Longings are the seat of our passion. They are the heart's desires. They are the sighs too deep for words. They are the silent gasps of prayer. They are the *oohs* and the *aahs*. They speak like a child. *Wow. Whoopee. Weeeeee!*

The Questions
What is my bliss? What gives me joy? What am I longing to do? To be? Why am I hesitating to follow my bliss? What are the obstacles in my way?

The Prayer
O God, let me live my longings. Let me know and name my dreams. Let me seize the moment and the day. Let me be alive to all of it. Let my faith flow like a current of grace. Amen.

The Calling

We are not permitted to choose the frame of our destiny. But what we put into it is ours.

—*Dag Hammarskold*

I am often asked the question, "When did you know that you were called to the ministry?" I wince at the question. I know people are looking for some burning bush experience. God never spoke to me out of a cloud. There was no lightning bolt. I saw no vision. My calling has been more a snowball rolling down a hill. Each year of ministry I pack more snow onto the ball. Each year I pick up more steam.

Anyone can be called. I suspect everyone is called. It may come as a whisper or a shout, a gentle touch or a push, a hunch or an answered prayer. The issue is whether we choose to take note. I believe the Spirit nudges the human spirit with messages of encouragement or warning, expressions of divine wishes, promptings to use our gifts, demands to expose our talents, a hint of how to become holy and happy at the same time.

My calling to ministry has been such a gradual unfolding. At the time I decided to enter Seminary, I took the following into consideration: I was a gifted speaker. I enjoyed people of all ages. I was thought to be compassionate and sensitive. I was also a big spiritual doubter. I was and am a perfectionist. I had a suspicion that organized religion had been doing more harm than good.

I hate to admit it, but my call was sealed when my Ping-Pong ball made me number 15 in the Vietnam draft. I had been leaning toward Seminary. Now I ran.

I was pleasantly surprised to find Seminary to be the perfect place for me. We studied subjects and topics that fascinated me. Classes in spirituality and pastoral counseling pried open whole new sides of me. My first encounter with Jesus the rebel and radical was, to say the least, an eye-opener. My fieldwork in local churches exposed me to their immense potential to do good. I became intrigued by the endless possibilities of ministry.

My calling has continued to unfold. I have grown not only in my ability to do the work of ministry, but my faith has gotten firmer and finer as well. I am more aware of God's abundant grace. Prayer comes more easily. I turn more over to God. I work every day to overcome my perfectionism. I can feel God poking and prodding me in certain directions. I pay attention. I listen up.

I have also come to realize that my calling is not just to my job. I, like everyone, am called to life. We are called to embrace life with an open mind and a full heart. We are commissioned by God to greet each day as a gift, to relax and enjoy it, to follow God's lead, to fill each day with love and laughter, to make hope happen, to create a miracle.

A calling is a belief. It is the belief that one is living in a manner pleasing to God. It is the surrendering of the human will to God's will. It is God's will for humans to be human. We are not called to be saints. This is not an unhappy surrender. This white flag waves with joy. A calling frees us to be the person we were meant to be, the individual God created us to be. God's Grace is the only burden we are asked to carry.

Gifted and Talented

I am not thrilled with American education these days. I hold that there are too many tests, too many rankings, too much competition. When I speak with parent and teacher groups, I remind them of the danger of labels—especially designating certain kids as gifted and talented. All kids are gifted and talented. What a disservice to make our children believe that only a few are worthy of that term.

Every Sunday during worship, we have a time allotted just for our children. If I ask the four- and five-year-olds to tell me what they are good at, I get hands waving madly. "I am good at soccer." "I can play the piano." "I am a good drawer." I have to make them stop answering. They wonderfully could go on and on. If I ask the eight-, nine-, and ten-year-olds the same question, I get downcast faces. There is a shouting silence. Fumes of embarrassment fill the air.

What happened? How do these kids learn so quickly to be awkward when asked about their abilities? Why do we make it so difficult for kids to claim their gifts or name their talents? Humility has its place, but so does confidence. So does the celebration of the myriad talents and gifts of our children. Our job as parents and pastors and teachers is to locate those talents and to provide opportunities for those gifts to be seen. We are to set the stage and run the spotlight. We need to be there to hand out the programs and be the first to stand in applause.

A gift is what comes naturally. It is something we do with relative ease. It is our inclination. It is a central feature of our being. It is whatever we do without having to do much work and, ironically, what we are most willing to work at doing. We may be a gifted singer or sewer. We may be able to hit the ball a mile or run one very fast. We may have excellent intuition or a kind heart. Our gifts are too many to mention, but each needs to be acknowledged.

A talent is what pleases others, what others choose to notice, or what is in fashion. We can be amply talented, yet have no audience, stage, or forum. A living faith asks us to see life as the stage. We are called to get up and strut our stuff on life's stage. Even if the theater is bare, if we listen hard enough and long enough, we will hear God cheering.

A Genius

My father was a simple man. He went to school until he was 14. He left England when he was 16 and headed for fame and fortune in America. He found neither. He was a cop and then a typewriter repairman. He married and had two kids. He made a decent living. He lived in

Racine, Wisconsin, the remainder of his fairly uneventful life. He enjoyed sitting on the front porch with a pipe full of tobacco. He died in a nursing home where they cared exclusively for Alzheimer's patients.

At his funeral, one of my high school buddies came up to me and said, "Your dad had a genius for making us all feel like a million bucks." I was speechless. It was true. All my childhood friends sought out my dad for the pat on the back or the glowing compliment. Dad bragged about every kid in the neighborhood. He had something good to say about each and every child he met.

Our front porch was often the setting for a gathering of kids and teenagers. It was there that my father held court. He had no learned degrees, no earthshaking insights, no mind-boggling ideas to share. He simply told each of us that we were the best. If we struck out, we were sure to get a hit the next time. If we flunked the test, the test was stupid. If we had disappointed our parents, they would love and forgive us anyway. His message was consistent. My father was a genius at dispensing grace.

It doesn't take a genius to figure out the secret to a good life. It is filling that life with positive energy. It is looking for and finding the good in one another. It is having faith that God is at work in each of us and our world. It is a faith alive with hope. It is a faith grounded in grace.

I think it is important to note here that my father was never able to acknowledge or affirm any relationship to God.

I never heard him utter a phrase that would qualify as an expression of faith. The fact remains that God worked in him and through him. God works most often in spite of us, not because of us. We may never know we've been called until others inform us we were an answered prayer.

The Questions
What are my gifts? What are my talents? To what am I called?

The Prayer
O God, we give thanks for the blessing of gifts and talents. May we name them and claim them. May we celebrate them. May we rejoice in lifting them up in your name. May they be used in your gracious service. Amen.

Miracle-Making

Where there is great love, there are always miracles.
—*Willa Cather* (Death Comes for the Archbishop)

Miracles are gifts from God. They are expressions of pure grace. Miracles reveal the nature of life—and God beheld that it was all very good. They reveal human nature—we are blessed to the core of our being. They reveal God's nature—love that could melt the sun.

Miracles can also be a choice. They can be the result of creating a context conducive to their reception. They can be the consequence of something as simple as an open eye or heart or mind or something as complex as having to be at the right place at the right time.

Miracles can also be created. They are the fruit of the human will working harmoniously with the Divine will. They are the harvest of a soul searching daily for the holy. Ironically, they are often the aftermath of tragedy. Paradoxically, they are epiphanies released from the grave, which feel as if they were sent from above.

Miracles can be huge and utterly transforming. They can be minute and only slightly adjust our spiritual position. They can be loud or soft. They can caress or slap. They can come out of nowhere or everywhere. They can be witnessed alone or a in a throng.

Miracles leave us dumbstruck but wiser. They take our breath away, but fill us with spiritual energy. They leave us speechless, but give us our faith vocabulary. We cannot explain miracles, but we also cannot stop talking about them.

A living faith can make a miracle. How? I believe it to be similar to gardening: If we have found rich soil that has access to abundant light and water and a gardener who is ready and willing to weed and fertilize, the seeds will come. The divine is showering the earth with seed on a moment-to-moment basis.

Rich Soil

We know rich soil. We know how it looks, how it feels, and even how it smells. The same is true of the soul. We know when it is ready to grow a miracle and when it is not.

The soul is not ready to grow a miracle when we are uptight and overstressed, burned out and up, or sick and tired. We are soil as dry as dust, choked by weeds, rocky and rootless.

When we are working feverishly to control our lives, too busy to bother with what truly matters, too consumed in making money to have time for God, life will leave us high and dry. We become poor soil that is as hard as rock and tough as nails, soil without moisture, soil in which nothing can grow.

When we are relaxed, at ease, calm, and in balance, we are rich soil. When we are productive yet at peace, firm but flexible, worry-free, and full of faith, we are soil moist with grace and ready for planting. A miracle is ready in the wings, waiting to take root.

Making a miracle is all about attitude. Being positive is a statement of faith. It states that we are positive that God is present. It speaks of God's obvious creative work in our lives. It is the assurance that if we are open to it, God will plant a miracle in our lives this very day.

Making a miracle is also a matter of perspective. If it is true that seeing is believing, it is equally true that many times believing is seeing. If faith is our lens, we can see the handiwork of God. Through God's eyes, all of life is witnessed as a miracle. For a living faith, life becomes a fireworks spectacular of miracles. We are left *oohing* and *aahing* and waiting for the grand finale.

Water and Light

It is the soul that will receive the miracle. It is the soul that will be transformed by the contents of the miracle. It is the soul that will be informed of the miracle's meaning.

The making of a miracle is readying the soul to receive. This is done in three primary ways: silence, stillness, and solitude. The soul must be at ease and well rested. Just as a baby quiets before the rigors of birth, a soul must find peace before it is ready for birthing a miracle.

Silence frees us from noise, from the din of a demanding world, from the expectations of our family and friends. Silence waters the soul. The soul becomes moist, ready to absorb a miraculous message, ready to hear the Word of God. Miracles are written in the hand of the Word of God.

Stillness allows the frenzy of our lives to cease. The spinning stops. The rush is over. The busyness halts. Calm is restored. Like the eye of a hurricane, here the spiritual weather is magnificent. There is bright sun and blue sky. The miracle happens in the eye, in the stillness, in the light.

Solitude is the absence of others, of their needs and worries and fears, and even their happiness and joys. Solitude is the absence of others and all else. This absence creates the space to receive the Presence of God. Solitude is sacred space, a place where God can gain access to our souls. God enters our soul via the passageway of solitude. Solitude is the stable behind the barn. There is room for God there.

God the Gardener fills this space with bright light that will make the seeds yearn for release and growth. God waters the soul with water of newness and hope that goes deep to our spiritual roots, fueling the buds and blossoms of faith so they might crawl to the surface.

Weeding and Fertilizing

Making a miracle requires a soul of strength and character. The soul must have a big back and a sturdy spine. The soul must be unafraid of tackling difficult issues, willing to face conflict and pain, and possessed of sufficient courage to ride the roller coaster of life.

Miracles are grown in rich soil. Rich soil requires plenty of fertilizing manure. Manure for the soul comes in the form of suffering, service, and sacrifice.

Suffering is on life's menu. It is a main course. There is no escaping its bitter taste. The making of a miracle enables us to find meaning in our suffering. Our losses tenderize our hearts. Our broken hearts and dreams remind us that we are the glue for one another. Our grieving locates our earth and heavenly angels. Our tears fertilize our faith. A living faith transforms suffering from bitter to bittersweet.

Service is often the response to suffering. Suffering creates compassion. Compassion creates the desire to help others. The great suffering caused by the tragic events of September 11 created a remarkable opportunity for service. Folks flocked to serve. Kindness gushed. Good deeds rose out of the ashes to a height far surpassing those of the Towers. A miracle of love happened. Spirits were reignited. Souls warmed. Life returned.

The greatest miracles of all may ride piggyback on genuine sacrifice. When we choose to give up that which we cherish and do so solely for the benefit of another, a miracle is bound to occur. We are stunned by genuine generosity. We are blown away.

When the human spirit forfeits its own desire to meet the needs of another, we are most Godlike. We truly reflect the Grace of God. Miracles have been dabbed onto our lives like the dots on a connect-the-dot picture. At first they appear random. As we mature and gain in wisdom, we begin to connect the dots. The connections begin to establish an outline. It is a face. The face of God begins to emerge. For each of us, the face is unique. No two faces are the same. Each face is alive with love and laughter. Each miraculous face beams with hope.

The Questions
What miracles were dabbed onto my childhood? Adolescence? Adulthood? How have these miracles shaped and formed my faith?

The Prayer
O God, what gifts you have given us! We are created in your image. We are co-Creators. We have hearts that can hold mysteries, minds that can work magic, and souls that can make miracles happen. We are most wonderfully made. Amen.

Afterword

Faith is a pure grace. It is a gift. It is the present.

The quest to discover our faith is a journey of joy. It is a pilgrimage back to our soul. It is a return trip to our essence. Discovering our faith is, more often than not, a process of recovering and uncovering. It is finding a faith we have lost, or discarded, or allowed to fade into the background of our lives. It is coming back home to the God who patiently waits for us. It is the coming full circle—from alpha to omega.

This little book has sought to show us how to find faith. How to listen closely to our lives. How to pay attention to the messages of our bodies. How to see inside our days. How to notice the miracles in the mundane. How to lift up the extraordinary out of the ordinary. How to choose to be aware, awake, and alert. How to ready ourselves to receive and rejoice in the gift of the moment.

Faith is all about receiving it. It is about opening our ears and eyes, our hearts and minds, our souls and spirits. It is about cracking open the tough nut the world has helped us to create, breaking through the images and masks that we wear to keep everyone happy, and revealing the real self, the delightfully human, the mysteriously divine.

Faith is all about freedom. The freedom to be. To be human. To get off the demoralizing treadmill of perfectionism. To leave the stage of performance. To walk away from the ways of the world. To declare our understanding of God. To leave a trail which is our fifth Gospel. To keep moving. Ahead. Beyond. Upward.

Faith is our original blessing. It is our essence, our core. It is solid as a rock. It is as fluid as a river. It is grounded, and it flows. It has deep roots, and it can fly. It is of the earth and the heavens. The seed of faith was planted in us at our birth. It is in our maturation that we blossom as flowers of God. Each a bouquet. Each a magnificent gathering of weed, wild, and beauty.

Most of all, I hope you found in these pages the inspiration to celebrate, to celebrate the gift of who you are, to see your faith as worthy and wondrous, to know that you are beloved, chosen, and adored by God, to know that God is enough. You are enough. Your faith is enough. For today, all is enough. Tomorrow, the transformation begins. The freshness explodes. All things become new. Your faith, like mine, is on the road again ….